Home Front

poems by

Anne Johnson Mullin

Finishing Line Press
Georgetown, Kentucky

Home Front

dedicated to my cousin, Marlyn McGrath Lewis, whose visits to our grandparents' house did not begin until after World War II had become history. Here's a bit of what she missed.

Copyright © 2020 by Anne Johnson Mullin
ISBN 978-1-64662-166-8 First Edition
All rights reserved under International and Pan-American Copyright Conventions.
No part of this book may be reproduced in any manner whatsoever without written permission from the publisher, except in the case of brief quotations embodied in critical articles and reviews.

ACKNOWLEDGMENTS

"Embers" and "Love Song to My Father" appeared in *Off the Coast*

"Language of Chairs" appeared in *Animus* and *Surface Tension*

"Snapshot", "Strong Box" and "Confidence" appeared in *Common Ground Review*

Publisher: Leah Maines
Editor: Christen Kincaid
Cover Art: Anne Johnson Mullin
Author Photo: Sharon Ann Aicher
Cover Design: Elizabeth Maines McCleavy

Printed in the USA on acid-free paper.
Order online: www.finishinglinepress.com
also available on amazon.com

Author inquiries and mail orders:
Finishing Line Press
P. O. Box 1626
Georgetown, Kentucky 40324
U. S. A.

Table of Contents

- Storied 1
- On the Wing 2
- Routine 4
- Difference 5
- Learning Curve 6
- Boys 7
- Service 8
- Sacrifice 9
- Words to That Effect 10
- Classified 11
- Goosey 12
- The Bed 13
- Home Front 14
- 30-Year Mortgage 15
- Civil but Strange 16
- Embers 17
- Here's Your Hat. What's Your Hurry? 18
- The Beaters 19
- Under Silence 20
- Sweet 21
- Strong Box 22
- Love Song to My Father 23
- Snapshot 24
- Leaving 25
- Women's Club 26
- Strings 27
- Hope 28
- Legacy 29
- Confidence 30
- Just Fine 31
- Language of Chairs 32

Author's Statement

World War II had so many heroes serving in all branches of the U.S. military and supporting it. So many families suffered disruption and losses. So many loved ones did not return, or, if they did, they were broken.

My own family's experiences during 1942 – 1945 were hardly the stuff of heroic chronicles. But memories that stayed with me for all the years since I was five continue to surprise me. Perhaps millions of us who were not impacted directly, who never thought of ourselves as heroic in any way, were affected more by "the duration" than we realized.

Yes, there was an undercurrent of fear based on spotty information, propaganda and rumors. There was suspicion of foreigners from Europe and Asia (who might be enemy spies!) There were shortages of consumer goods, rationing of food and gasoline, but essentially a good-hearted sense of "we're all in this together" prevailed. These poems are meant as a tribute to that long-ago-spirit of the Home Front.

Storied

the house we knew
was built from stories old
before anyone showed us
stones under the cellar
when roto-rooter men dug
to free drainage pipes

no accident we call them stories
they tell of beginnings before
we enter at our own level
ready to climb narrow stairs
to the attic where we find
an old opera hat holding
what remains of a mouse

death is an old story and
hard to learn but origins
are harder to follow
beneath roots of roots
the house that told us
our earliest stories is the one
we dwell in always . . .

On the Wing

May 1942 we moved in
with my grandparents for
the duration which is what
adults called the war
I awoke that first morning
in the small bedroom
third floor rear now mine
from the window
I looked up at the
underside of eaves
down on roofs
of back porches
flowering trees
a man trundling
his wheelbarrow
in a field next door

***

during that war
we all lived together
under the erratic roof
that jolted soft layers
of sky and flights of pigeons
at night we peered through
cracks in drawn black shades
to watch neighbors with
Civil Air Patrol armbands
my mother among them
guarding the streets below

***

the pet canary found
on its back on the
newsprint lining the
bottom of the cage
taught something
about death but not
enough to know
how to unlearn
lifeless ounces of
tiny bones and feathers
consigned to an envelope
sealed for burial
the idea of tragedy
forever on the wing

***

grownups huddled
around radio broadcasts
after my bedtime I couldn't
make out their words but
the smoke drifting
up the stairwell from
Grandfather's pipe bore
an aroma of comfort

***

over the blackened dome
of the statehouse seconds away
airplanes droned above
blankets of darkness
the nighthawk's cry
that circled through sleep
echoes still

Routine

shafts of yellow sun illuminate
dust motes escaping from the
brown velveteen sofa cushions

my mother sinks into after hours
on her feet as a bank teller replacing
Joyce Larkin's father deployed to Italy

she is grateful for tea her mother brings
but agrees enough afternoon sun
remains for coasting at the playground

up the street and around two corners
where the slope begins to grow slick
under lengthening shadows

snow clots our mittens   cuffs   insides
of overshoes with cold I never feel
until later tramping home past windows

whose blue or gold stars honoring
family warriors are now darkened
shades pulled against escaping light

Difference

Miss Weddleton was
our first-grade teacher

she stood at the blackboard
to show us how to form letters

but we were more than forty
children who couldn't see much

beyond each other   the difference
between "b" and "d" eluded us

something about the loop
at the bottom of the stick

going to the right or the left
Miss Weddleton yelled a lot

she was worried and nervous
because her fiancé flew airplanes

that dropped bombs in Europe
my mother told me   Erika Wechter

with her long wool stockings and
pale skin joined our class in January

from Austria she might have
told us about air raids if we had

known enough to ask   on Fridays
we brought quarters to school

fit them into cardboard folders
we thought we were buying

savings bonds   we had
no idea we were buying bombs.

Learning Curve

one recess Charlotte Conroy who was bigger than
most of us in first grade said she would show us
a new game   we had to line up   all the jews
over here   all the christians over there   some of us
weren't sure if catholics belonged with the christians
or not but Charlotte said we did

Charlotte told us that the jews had killed Jesus
a shock because we had learned in sunday school
to blame Pontius Pilate   then she said
the christian group should be ready to fight
the "dirty jews" right there on the playground
when she gave the order

which she never did because Miss Weddleton
on yard duty had heard enough to grab Charlotte
by the arm and yell at us all   *did we not know
that JESUS HIMSELF was a JEW* another shock
we were sure that Jesus belonged in our church
because his statue was there

*did we not know that this very WAR was
being fought because NAZIS were KILLING JEWS
that Charlotte's behavior was EVIL for spreading HATE*
what we did know was fear as Charlotte was marched
to the principal's office and we learned our parents
would be informed of our *shameful participation*

but first Miss Weddleton had us all shake hands and
apologize to each other   hugs were ok and tears
at home that night there was serious talk about differences
between religious beliefs and churches and temples
my mother called some of the others who agreed to
treat Miss Weddleton to lunch next Saturday

Boys

on the backs of their arithmetic papers
checked for accuracy and returned by our teacher
boys drew airplanes with swastikas or
rising sun circles on the wings and flames
spiraling downward

sometimes they drew tanks and battleships
with zig-zag lines and puffy rings
to show bursts of anti-aircraft fire
aimed upward at doomed enemy pilots
with savage buck-toothed grimaces

boys passed them secretly by reaching
under their seats or wadding them to drop
on each other's desks when they went
to the pencil sharpener mounted on
a back corner wall

girls weren't considered worthy viewers but
sometimes Michael Berman who sat behind me
showed me what he had been scratching over
sucking in saliva with effort and making
ack-ack-sounds under his breath

nobody had television yet so movie newsreels and
Life magazine must have fueled all that graphic violence
or maybe it's just a boy thing because in the '70s
my sons with our German exchange students sketched
down-spouting hueys over jungles

Service

some fathers went
into the service which
made them heroes

my father was just
a year too old and
hard of hearing

Joanie Keating's dad
had brand new teeth
when he came home

Dolly O'Leary's brother
did not come home
never knew his son

my uncle took his law degree
to Washington and served
in the quartermaster corps

when he came home on leave
bringing prime steaks
unavailable to civilians

Grandmother was delighted
to broil and serve them
but Grandfather and

my father chose to eat sandwiches
of processed cheese spread
for dinner that night

Sacrifice

so you stomped on tin cans
to flatten them   bundled
newspapers and magazines

counted ration book coupons
and tokens   calculated to see if
there were enough for meat   milk

margarine came uncolored
in plastic pillows with a bead of dye
to pinch then knead and maybe toss

back and forth with your father until
the time you missed   splattered the floor
your mother blamed your dad

you did not miss bubblegum that much
plastic worked ok for roller skates and
the bugle you learned on for school band

no one bought new cars or drove
anywhere just for fun   even so
you learned nothing about sacrifice

until pale shy children from Peking
Vienna and Jerusalem with odd
clothes and haircuts

and mothers who looked older than yours
were placed in your classroom
and taught you

Words to that Effect

DON'T YOU KNOW THERE'S A WAR ON?
the question you heard all around you from

the counter girl at the Dorothy Muriel bakery
who ran out of cupcakes

the driver of an already overloaded bus
pulling away from a furious crowd

a gas station owner with limited supply and a long
line of cars pulling in

characters on the Jack Benny or Duffy's Tavern or Allen's Alley
radio shows on any pretext whatsoever

the lunchroom ladies if they caught you throwing away
perfectly good food while starving children in Europe had none

your teacher if you failed to use both sides of the paper
your own mother if you whined about spam—again

Classified

Uncle Eddie's army friend Gino flew
on reconnaissance missions in Italy to
photograph possible landing sites and
monitor enemy troop movements and
although I didn't understand all that
it was exciting when the mail brought
a large brown envelope addressed to me
with lots of colorful stamps and glossies
of fields and mountains and kids
with toothy smiles swinging their legs
from the hood of an odd-looking car and
Gino with some other guys in tee shirts
lounging on stone steps and smoking

Gino wrote a brief note saying I might
like to bring the pictures to school
to show my second- grade class but
my parents were afraid that might get
Gino or all of us in trouble even though
the photos showed no street signs or
army insignia or major buildings that
could be considered classified information
and besides Uncle Eddie said that
Gino would never have sent anything risky

I was encouraged to write pen-pal letters
to Gino but my parents hid the photos
kyboshing my aspirations of being a
big cheese in Mrs. Lovejoy's class
you can't be too careful they fretted
Gino sent a couple more notes and photos
but then the envelopes stopped coming
I was afraid to ask what had happened
I knew nobody would tell me the truth until
they thought I was old enough to hear it

Goosey

realtors call them Victorian Ladies
three-storied gabled structures housing
two homes of one and a half floors each
my grandparents had bought the first one
built on that block of St. Paul Street

in the '40s their tenants were the Dimmits
a dentist always referred to as The Doctor
and his wife Dell whose son Phil was away
at college trying for a draft deferment

evenings when The Doctor was in
his easy chair cigar smoke writhed through
the downstairs apartment door into the shared
vestibule   *C'mon in—don't be strangers*
he would hail anyone who passed
rattling the ice in his highball as a cue
for Dell to fill his glass as she played hostess

grownups I was with usually demurred
escaping The Doctor's ebullience for our
more subdued family quarters upstairs but
once Grandfather and I did stop in to say
hello to Dell's mother Mrs. Delano on her
semi-annual visit from "M'zoora"

peering through her lorgnette Mrs. D suggested
that Grandfather should create a rose arbor
by the back door and also train honeysuckle up
the front porch pillars as her gardener in St. Louis
had done *Oh, and perhaps he could add a fountain?*
Grandfather said he would consider the matter

which he did later at our dining table . . . *she may
have all the dough in that family, but she sure is
a silly goose*   from then on but only upstairs
Mrs. Delano was The Goose or Goosey for short

The Bed

after The Doctor retired and the Dimmits
moved back to Missouri they left behind
the six-foot-high head and foot boards
plus side rails all solid maple with
spiral carved posts framing panels
whose centers hold hex-like designs

Grandfather gave the bed to my husband and me
for our first house but on moving day when
our new staircase proved too tight to accommodate
its bulk my spouse dared to saw six inches
off the legs to be re-attached later

we could not have known how many years and
children and moves that quick fix would withstand
I still polish the spirals and hex signs
we still sleep soundly

Home Front

in daylight until darkness demanded
we pull our black window shades before
turning on the lights inside we could see
Mary next door in her top floor workroom
stitching satin ruching and rosettes
wrapping silk panels around wire frames

lampshades were her business solitary
labor that suited a timid personality
but when my mother agreed to be a
Civil Air Patrol warden for our block
Mary also volunteered she almost fainted
my mother said when they had to practice
the fireman's carry and Mary drew
a burly male partner

she passed the hands-on training
wore her badge and walked the street
by low-beam flashlight during air raid drills
years later as her father grew more frail
and ill she cared for him with skills
practiced on the home front

30- Year Mortgage

in 1945 the final payment
all of us gathered around
the lace-tablecloth dinner
to celebrate in spite of rationing
one more freedom

Grandmother recalls
she was the one who met
with the banker to answer
all the questions about
a down payment about
selling the old row house
where she had taken in roomers
about renting out half the new Victorian
to meet the monthly payments
her husband's salary as a fireman
could not quite cover

in 1915 the loan in her name meant
that before Americans trooped to Europe
in that earlier war my mother and
her younger brother played catch
in the back yard at 105 St. Paul Street
careful not to trample newly planted iris
careful not to disturb the tenants
careful not to act like wild Irish kids
who could ruin a neighborhood
that was not yet safe for democracy

Civil but Strange . . .

. . . a motto my grandparents
lived by they were not
intimate with their neighbors
hello or *nice day* sufficed
for conversation somehow
they learned that Victor
whose small orchard
abutted their back corner
had immigrated from
his native Italy just
before the war with
enough money to buy
the house and land
he cultivated working
long hours in his baggy
overalls and battered
brown felt hat

our family wondered
how did he make a living
did he sell his produce
maybe on the black market
could he be some kind of spy

once in a while a paper bag
full of plums or pears
appeared on our back porch
and the next time
Grandfather saw Victor
he would wave and
shout *thank you*
Victor would doff his hat
and that was that

Embers

Grandfather ordered time by tasks
winding the hall clock brushing his
uniforms polishing his badge
he was a fireman always dutiful
at the station he coiled hose
shined hardware timed practice drills
once he let me slide down the pole

when the Liggett's drugstore burned
the site smoldered acrid and sickly sweet
for days I tried not to picture him
in the brown smoke chunks of walls
and water falling

stay back he warned me against
the heat when he tended the furnace
at home the upper door clanked
as he unhasped it and stabbed
long shovelfuls of coal from the bin
deep into the maw of flames that roared
orange fury flickering within
whitewashed walls

mornings from the low trap door
he'd shovel out dead ash and clinkers
leavings of a deadly conflagration
I knew he would always
protect me from

years later selling his house I lead
the real estate agent down flights
of stairs to inspect the new oil burner
installed just months before he died
I still taste coal dust

Here's Your Hat. What's Your Hurry?

that line from a vaudeville skit
would bring my father and grandfather
to guffaws they relished not just
the joke but the shared laughter
which came easily now between them
and made them forget how
at first they had been strangers
one a stocky veteran firefighter
used to confronting danger the other
a sensitive artist who had somehow
enchanted my mother and proven
worthy by the time I witnessed
the way they worked together
in the kitchen after family dinners
one washing the other drying
my father singing Shuffle Off
to Buffalo and my grandfather doing
soft-shoe routines both of them
warned by their spouses to be careful
with the good china and each of them
anticipating the other's next move
as if having discovered how many
Keith's Vaudeville Circuit acts
they could approximate together
they did not worry about
the curtain coming down

The Beaters

three oriental patterned carpets
from the living and dining rooms
plus hallway runners required
my grandfather and father to
team up for seasonal beatings

as one raised the legs of sofas
dining room table and sideboard
the other jerked the rugs out
both bent over to roll and
then heft the burden around
corners of doorways and
banisters neither of them able
to see his own feet feeling for
the steps counting down
four flights to the back yard
and a final heave up and over
cable stretched between poles

barely recharged these two
kindly even-tempered men
took turns beating with the wire loop
raised dirt that grimed their faces
whaled the hell out of all that was
wrong with the world
strong enough to laugh at folly
climbing back up steep stairs

Under Silence

for vacation we all went by train
from Boston to Yarmouth on Cape Cod
with piles of luggage and the birdcage
draped to calm Tippy the canary
then by bus to Eastham where
the cottage we rented was owned
by the Collins family whose son
was serving in the Pacific Fleet
nights in Eastham were quiet and dark
no drivers on the road no lights showing
from other cottages no voices or loud
radios no screen doors slamming
silence so clear you could hear
the three-note whip-poor-will
moths strumming window screens
often the coughs and soft mutters of
Bernie Collins' lobster boat taking him
out maybe to fish for bass or to notify
the U.S. Coast Guard if he saw any
suspicious enemy craft in the area
always under it all the thunder
of surf pounding the beaches
of Wellfleet and Truro nearby and
Normandy too we learned later

Sweet

summer neighbors on the Cape
the Azvest sisters from New Jersey
vacationed at a grueling pace
depending on the tide they rowed out
at dawn to fish for flounder or dig
for quahogs later they foraged
for berries then spent afternoons
baking pies and simmering vats of
beach plums or blackberries for jam
escaping for a swim in the cove
while their steamy kitchen cooled
before they started cooking dinner
all their sweetness required more sugar
than the monthly ration books allowed
so my mother and grandmother
quietly exchanged shares of their
allotment of five-pound bags for
samples of fresh-baked bounty
when Grandfather worried aloud
about the shrinking level in our
sugar bowl Grandmother was quick
to cajole illogically *Ed we could all
use less in our tea and on our cereal
now how about another slice of
Marguerite's blueberry pie?*

Strong Box

tucked in with insurance policies
power of attorney notarized copies
of her parents' death certificates
pins rewarding meritorious years
of service at the Watertown Arsenal
my late aunt's safe deposit box
contains a spiral bound handful
of black and white snapshots
young men in dinner jackets
ties loosened hair slicked back
slim women there is
my youthful aunt herself
in a soft-draped skirt and
platform shoes with ankle straps
the party in full swing bottles
and loaded ashtrays on
white tablecloths everyone
playing to the camera

maybe he was one of them
the writer of faded letters
in thin envelopes folded
with the photos

We are still stuck here
in Wurtzburg, don't know
if we'll get sent to the Pacific.
Helen, I keep hoping
you will write.
     Al

Love Song for My Father

you sang every morning while you shaved
you began the beguine you danced
'til three under stars chilled by the winter
with your sleepy-time gal you didn't care
if smoke got in your eyes or laughing friends
derided you displayed that sugar cake
for all the boys to see in the small café
by the park across the way you admired
figures less than Greek the Eiffel Tower
the time of the Derby winner you ordered
seafood mama you toted and lifted
barge and bale you were no lazybones
sleepin' in the noonday sun

I would watch the high notes float out
perfectly from the tremble in your throat
through the rounds of your lathered lips
in the bathroom mirror you would lift me
so I could see us grinning at each other
no one has sung that way to me since

last night on the radio Joe Williams
extolled the million dollar baby
from the five and ten cent store
I was looking at the moon but
I was seeing you

Snapshot

the young army officer stands
in sunlight polished boots form
a precise angle hands behind his back
a bench set against one gnarled tree
invites repose beside a low wall
of stone blocks perhaps a garden
once grew in the space between
the wall and the man pinned
by the camera's lens

still pasted on the back of the photo
a yellowed newspaper clip identifies
Lieutenant Henry J. McGrath
of Brookline as the recipient of a
Distinguished Service Cross
"story to run 8/12/18 Thursday a.m."

no one could have known the soldier
would come back to a life with two or
three unhappy marriages too much
booze eventually no contact with
his oldest brother

in this picture my mother must have saved
 for almost eighty years no shadows
darken her Uncle Henry's handsome face.

Leaving

Grandmother's only brother
left Boston in the 1890s for labor in
New York and was never heard from again
my mother couldn't tell me what happened
or why her mother had barely mentioned it
he might have been killed in a construction
accident or some kind of gang trouble
common back then was all she was told

in contrast Grandfather's youngest sister
Mildred left to marry a California man
who owned blocks of San Francisco
her siblings kept close track named
daughters after her vied with each other
to be remembered in her will by this
childless very wealthy widow who
outlived them all except Grandfather
she left him a windfall of blue chip stocks

I used to hear a lot about Mildred
met her once when she came east
swathed in mink tottering on thin legs
after a few martinis but knowing what
money has to do with everything does not
explain the stony acceptance under which
my grandmother buried the loss of her brother
whose name my mother thought was
William she wasn't sure
who simply left

Women's Club

it was about raising money
for scholarships for local girls
through monthly luncheons
rummage sales and occasional
drama productions one of the
youngest members my mother
in her forties played a leading role
one spring as a spunky teenager

on stage she was someone
I almost knew from family stories
about how she had won permission
to bob her hair and thus risk
being thought a tramp and then
to transfer from the academy run
by the sisters of St. Joseph
to the local high school to learn
to drive and repair and then buy
a Ford flivver by working
at a local bank instead of
going to college

I watched her perform as
someone daring and funny
someone I might become
but did not expect to find
at home again once
the show was over

Strings

flipping open the case
my mother once showed me
the violin cushioned in blue velvet
her father used to play when
they had family concerts . . .

often on Sunday evenings Auntie May
and her husband Francis he had
a beautiful voice would come over
with Frankie Jr. and Lucille then
after coffee and dessert
we all gathered at the piano
when I was able to play well enough
I could sit in for May at the old
upright Baldwin in the parlor. . .

I envied those family members
I would never meet who had known
my mother when she was my age and
who got together to generate music
I could only hear in a story told
just once before the leather case was
snapped shut and sold to strangers

Hope

because our teacher
required us to observe
and report signs of spring

we noticed on the walk to school
thin green sprouts of chicory
cracking through asphalt

hard to imagine what
came before the rupture
of dark confinement

by the merest filament
probing for light through tar
too young to be stymied

by logic we believed what
we saw we knew something
about hope we could not name

something about birth its force
we had lived through but
could not remember

Legacy

the small writing desk
has stood in a corner
of my living room
so many years and yet
I never thought to question
its source

my mother mentioned
it had been a wedding gift
to her mother but who
the donor or the maker
might have been
if she ever said
I don't recall

yesterday's annual straightening
unearthed stale correspondence
mismatched notecards
batches of recent photographs
and my mother's old address book

bearing names of people also
deceased no one I realized
surprised at the sudden sense
of loss to ask about the desk
rhe legacy of death includes
questions never asked
and so unanswered

Confidence

once I could tell you absolutely
the iris from Grandmother's garden
were the cream and magenta ones
with dark mink beards

too many moves and transplants later
I am not so sure

perhaps the lemon yellow their fragrance
evocative of visits to the St. Paul Street house
on June afternoons

or the tallest blue the color of her eyes
which gave back all I confided and more
even after a stroke spared her spirit
but not her speech

her clear gaze fostered confidence
in a sense beyond words every time
I told her what worried me about
a new job or getting married
pregnant or moving away

she would nod and pat my hand
which meant she understood
but was sure everything
would be all right

sometimes if she tried to say more
but couldn't she would shrug
never mind

Just Fine

then you were alone your husband dead
closets gone through clothes given away
notes written all those who had helped
returned to their own lives I'll be fine
you said I believed you

you were always the manager you did
the driving kept the checkbook
scheduled each day so when you said
you found it hard to know what to do
without Daddy I could not believe you

he always made the decisions
you said but I knew otherwise
whatever you think best, Marion
he'd whistle working at his drawing board
needing reminders that dinner was ready

if you had told me you ached
for his singing his warmth
waltzing you around the kitchen
I would have understood but I
had to learn how loss distorts reality

you told me you were beginning to
enjoy lunches with friends to think about
a new car you said I shouldn't worry
because you were fine I said I was too
we were mother and daughter after all

Language of Chairs

nothing so
eloquent as a chair
wrapped
around absence saying
all there is to say
about loss

chairs are words
presenting speakers who
are not here but whose breath
brushes our ears and
softens our lips

we cannot always
hear or see clearly
what is real we need
to grip edges to define
meanings and ends

arms and laps held us
when we were afraid of words
that fell like bombs words
we could not understand
life everlasting

Anne Johnson Mullin was born in Boston in 1937. Her experience of World War II began in 1942, when she and her parents moved in with her grandparents, where they spent the next three years, a time of "indelible" memories, she notes.

Years later she earned her B.A. degree in English from Tufts University. Many more years later, she earned her M.A. from the University of Maine and her Ph.D. from the University of Massachusetts. Anne taught composition and directed the Writing Center at Idaho State University in Pocatello, home to a lively and supportive writing community.

Anne's career also included serving for many years as the Alumni Director at the University of Maine at Farmington, and as a humor columnist for the *Transcript Press* (Westwood, MA), *Harvard Football News*, and the *Franklin Journal* (Farmington, ME).

Her poems have appeared in the *Atlanta Review, Comstock Review, Puckerbrush Review, Off the Coast, Goose River Anthology,* and *Common Ground Review*. Finishing Line Press has previously published two of her chapbooks, *Surface Tension* and *Sometimes a Sonnet*.

Currently, Anne and her husband, Kevin, live in Bonita Springs, FL. They have four grown "children" and ten grandchildren.

www.ingramcontent.com/pod-product-compliance
Lightning Source LLC
LaVergne TN
LVHW041601070426
835507LV00011B/1232